THE LAW AND THE GRACE

THE LAW
AND THE GRACE

IAIN CRICHTON SMITH

1965
EYRE & SPOTTISWOODE
LONDON

First published in 1965 by
Eyre & Spottiswoode (Publishers) Ltd
22 Henrietta Street, London, WC2
© 1965 by Iain Crichton Smith
Printed in Great Britain by
Clarke, Doble & Brendon Ltd

CONTENTS

ACKNOWLEDGMENTS

Some of the poems in this collection have already appeared in print and acknowledgment is due to Scotland's Magazine for *At Tiumpan Head, Lewis*. *Johnson in the Highlands* and *Old Woman* have been read on the BBC Third Programme and *Old Highland Lady Reading Newspaper* has been read on the BBC Scottish Home Service. *Two Girls Singing* has been published in the *Glasgow Herald*.

AT THE RESERVOIR

I sat beside you on the stone stair.
Live flies bounced from the dead flies' backs.
The water was ominously bare
and flat and cold. We watched how Jack's
body arched through the air

down to the whiteness of a fish
where minute trout swarmed out and in
the colour of his live flesh
moving beyond us through the grin
of flat water threatening us.

And suddenly I thought that you
had arched and plummeted as well
into those depths I never knew
by any intellectual skill
and there where round us foxgloves grew

was writhing with an enmity
of the shuddering fish and bleak cold
till I clutched your arm lest my sky
should turn us over where we rolled
under the waters brutishly

both you and I and him we saw
cleaving the perfume of the dead
the foxgloves which the waters gnaw.
I clutched you till your shaken head
steadied to honey and to straw.

THIS BLUE CAULDRON

This blue cauldron of a stunned cold
boils below me. I look deeply down
past habit and dishonour and my skin
nagged by a wind that's testing every fold.

Arena beyond shadow, dense corrie
of ridged walls, terrible eyeball, I
see you now more bitter than the sky.
Deer would throttle here in the fiery

iron vice of blue, this clamped hole:
antlers sink where cormorants cartwheel
in an old gossip of the sunken gull.
Deer would, spitted on this hard pole,

in cold, in fire, turn, slowly turn,
this arcady of brine, these leaves of ice
where now I see as in a loving vice
two small brown ducks perched on a nest of iron.

AT TIUMPAN HEAD, LEWIS

I looked out across the water,
a few ducks, miles and miles of sea,
sparkling so coldly and so brilliantly
I almost fell into their mineral laughter

so clear, so cold, so passionate, so bright,
as a mind at the centre of all things.
Inhuman axis laughing, mill of wings.
The ducks fly on above that appetite

O iron-hard yet gentle. Consistent laughter
and wheel of love. Blue roses freeze and burn
in such great heat of cold, in such an iron
almost aloof delightedness of water.

MEETING

'They threw stones at me,' the old man said.
'They were some pupils from your school.'
I twitched with anger. What was I expected
to do for him, since I myself had cruel

intimations of mortality?
I almost turned away. He touched my coat.
'Sir!' he said. 'Sir!' I whinnied at that cry.
An empty horror filled my throat.

Naked like a fine spiritual horse
jabbed by needles I turned back to him.
The mottled redness his intently hoarse
words thrust from became almost dim

and slated with a lead servility.
His stick, thrust through that sunset, was on fire
with some dread question. I felt some pity
but more than pity a vain desire

for peace out of my precariousness.
'I'd know them.' His obscene face writhed
with an agèd almost evil singleness.
Some helpless anger in my chest breathed

heavily. Why must it be like this,
this see-saw of the spirit? I turned away.
'I'll see,' I said, 'what can be done.' His voice
droned slavishly. I hated him. The fray

to which he'd called me made me angry with him
I felt my fingers tighten round my case
because I hated him and because I came
into my weakness, hateful, ominous.

OLD WOMAN

Your thorned back
heavily under the creel
you steadily stamped the rising daffodil.

Your set mouth
forgives no-one, not even God's justice
perpetually drowning law with grace.

Your cold eyes
watched your drunken husband come
unsteadily from Sodom home.

Your grained hands
dandled full and sinful cradles.
You built for your children stone walls.

Your yellow hair
burned slowly in a scarf of grey
wildly falling like the mountain spray.

Finally you're alone
among the unforgiving brass,
the slow silences, the sinful glass.

Who never learned,
not even aging, to forgive
our poor journey and our common grave

while the free daffodils
wave in the valleys and on the hills
the deer look down with their instinctive skills,

and the huge sea
in which your brothers drowned sings slow
over the headland and the peevish crow.

LIVING TOGETHER

So sensitive my fingers hardly
touched you without fear of flame
or prison for my trembling name.
That wasn't love and quite absurdly

I now ask withdrawing more
from the hot selves that fill this space
we wander through in nakedness.
Is this love that makes me spare

by my own tenderness these egoes
sprouting so rich from this rank ground?
Ravenous faces without sound
eat air for praise and like old eagles

walk in humility. Is love
gentle compulsion? I enquire
because I hate the tactful fire
in which self-mercies slowly move.

THE WITCHES

Coveys of black witches gather
at corners, closes.
Their thin red pointed noses
are in among the mash of scandal.

Poking red fires with
intense breath, hot as the imagined
rape riding the hot mind.
The real one was more moral

and more admirable because animal.
In an empty air they convene
their red, sad, envious, beaks. The clean
winter rubs them raw

in a terrible void, hissing
with tongues of winter fire.
Pity them, pity them. Dare
to ring them with your love.

TWO GIRLS SINGING

It neither was the words nor yet the tune.
Any tune would have done and any words.
Any listener or no listener at all.

As nightingales in rocks or a child crooning
in its own world of strange awakening
or larks for no reason but themselves.

So on the bus through late November running
by yellow lights tormented, darkness falling,
the two girls sang for miles and miles together

and it wasn't the words or tune. It was the singing.
It was the human sweetness in that yellow,
the unpredicted voices of our kind.

MINISTER

In a moral cage all his days,
in the soul's diamond dazzling all ways,
in all expectations fixed
and nailed to a white text

how strange that not once did he run
naked among naked stone
howling impoverishment but clung
through births, deaths, late marrying,

to wife, children. Through the rock
the mortal snake mortally struck.
The wooden pew's iron eyes
hollowed out his joyful Sundays.

OLD HIGHLAND LADY READING
NEWSPAPER

Grasping the newspaper in kneaded hands
in her ordered bed, the tablets at the side,
she slowly reads of all her friends who've died
in the black holds of the approaching islands

where the horses and the daffodils are dead,
unfashionable skirts have swirled away
down the Dutch cornfields and the fields of hay
into the numerous caves of her bald head

bent over print and old remorseless hands
grasping these deaths, the tombstones all in white
her eyes traverse with gritty appetite
in the slow justice of her mouth's small sounds.

SCHOOLROOM INCIDENT

Whose fault was this?
Her fault? My fault perhaps?
'I should not talk so much if I were you.'
Ironic threatening among the maps.
Why the paralysis

of my own mind in guilt?
Too, I suppose, sensitive. And so
I dream all night of Nazis in their boots.
'I should not talk.' They grow
vicious, slimly built,

lashing my more than dream.
We also know how girls
suffer such jackboots in their dress.
Some livid envy curls
in hair my iron combs.

And I, cold master, am
sensitive hypocrite. Here
I lie in bed on such a rack perhaps
as too tight hair
brings no conceiving calm

but German virgin in
a silver uniform.
The moon remembers desolate waste fires.
The ashen storm
is (I submit) both his and hers and mine.

LENIN

In a chair of iron
sits coldly my image of Lenin,
that troubling man
'who never read a book for pleasure alone.'

The germ inside the sealed train
emerged, spread in wind and rain
into new minds in revolution
seeming more real than had been

for instance Dostoevsky. No, I can
romanticise no more that 'head of iron'
'the thought and will unalterably one'
'the word-doer', 'thunderer', 'the stone

rolling through clouds.' Simple to condemn
the unsymmetrical, simple to condone
that which oneself is not. By admiration
purge one's envy of unadult iron

when the true dialectic is to turn
in the infinitely complex, like a chain
we steadily burn through, steadily forge and burn
not to be dismissed in any poem

by admiration for the ruthless man
nor for the saint but for the moving on
into the endlessly various, real, human,
world which is no new era, shining dawn.

THE ARGUMENT

Our world is not predestined. So he chose
or did not choose to argue, being him.
And I being me in an excited pose
argued for our destiny, the trim
tracks that contain us, but he all aflame

spoke of the clear nobility of the soul,
himself both proud and noble. I replied
with words imperfectly in my control
how the will drives us, we undeified
unfree even for honour. He from pride

repelled such low dishonour. I appealed
to his pure passion, in a passionate tone
as if myself were suffering from guilt
but he quite calmly answered: 'We are known
to no-one else.' I answered: 'The cold stone

suffers its gravity, and why should we
assume such freedom of the phantom skies.
We are a part of sad eternity.'
But he then honestly with flashing eyes
as if by grace and not the law replied:

'We are no stones. How could we speak of this
unvaried destiny if this were true?'
I did not listen to hypothesis
but watched his face where passion through and through
showed grace more varied than his reason know,

a coiling of the spirit working there,
a human anguish of the beating soul,
and knew at last, had I not known before,
the struggle's what we live by, not the whole
unknown completion. I could humbly kneel

to such humanity predestined too,
noble behaviour of the best we are,
restless and proud, to abstract passion true.
Some world takes notice of the best and rare
as I of him, a passion of our star.

CUAN FERRY

We looked out across the water
from Cuan Ferry, the house on the left side.
The ferry turned slowly on its rudder.
The hills were ringed with gold. My cold head

turned from the brown woods to the Atlantic
in its blue ultimate fury. We stared in awe
at the shouldering water as it hugely broke
a world of distance from each golden shoe.

SCHOOLROOM

My room is bare and has no pictures in it,
not baldheaded Shakespeare nor grained Milton nor
any other dignitary or poet.

Because I suppose there's no virtue in a picture.
It's a disguise of what is really there,
a sort of lie. Milton might have approved.

But nevertheless the walls are very bare
Should I disguise the cracks by some colour?
In 'Samson Agonistes' this wasn't done.

But in point of fact the walls were all pulled down.
Even for children should I have stained glass windows?
Or pointless lions in a pointless desert?

Or is it egotism to offer only myself,
a resounding voice in a resounding room,
as Milton again in his own 'Paradise Lost'?

1964 is come around
and the long chain of men toiling on
through yellowing newspapers to a red dawn.
The films too will switch on their sound

'Blighty' and 'Tipperary', 'The Long Trail'
and that raw sunset bitterly our own
where Owen, Rosenberg are sternly grown
into the social family of the crystal

while the red-faced generals topple red port
('They wouldn't take me. These were glorious days.')
All the CO's (both kinds) stand slow at gaze
across to Flanders, while on fields of sport

all England's ghosts, the missing cabinet, run
wicket to wicket, as in Cuba here
the toiling fleets head towards flat despair
against the rising power of the sun

its nightmare hydrogen and huge fire
which in dark trenches was for them a friend
but now bounces from water without end—
our Double Feature, 1964.

TO A THEOLOGIAN

In the world of Kierkegaard and Bonhoeffer
all language moves prophetically in fire,
The book blazes. Heaven is read as hell.

Young theologian, you cannot will
through clever glasses the incredible
sufferings of genius and weakness.

Linguistic rainbows born of cleverness
return at last to their original rays
of deadly white, intolerable flame

where in a crooked window, born of shame
these two intensely crumpled run our time
down melted iron. Incompletely fixed

are more than saints, more than religious text.
Foreshortened on its pain, each meagre form
leans like a picture in a thunderstorm.

SCHOOLTEACHER

Roman lady, in your distant gown,
aloof to all but children, I might ask
where all your bridges are, though your mask
is clearly Roman in a play of stone.

'Build me some roads,' I plead, 'make up new maps.
This Europe isn't coloured. Consuls cry
in flapping tents of cold eternity.
And children too have worn their children's caps

note-taking blindly. How the empires fade
is wild barbarians at 4 o'clock.
Prepare not eagles only on your rock.
Aloof hauteurs of sovereign parades

bred hummings in the east. Throw out your roads.
A swirl of gown along a marble hall
is too inhuman for their festival,
the snigger of their rigorous black gods.'

THE TWO CLOUDS

What has this to do with 'the good'?
Today I saw a scorpion cloud
all claws, all Roman. I might brood

forever on it and the black horse
that toiled behind it, all arched back and ears,
and never catching up. The skies rehearse

a Roman poison and a Roman cure.
But what has this to do with literature?
Two clouds together which are black and pure.

JOHNSON IN THE HIGHLANDS

A reasoning mind travels through this country.
In these sad wastes a Londoner by choice
sees water falling, and some meagre deer.

Examines with his tough reasoning mind
lochs, deer, and people: is not seduced
by Mrs Radcliffe's green hysteria

from a musical prose we've never once achieved,
whose fences cannot reach between the words
whose arguments are broken-backed with exile.

A classical sanity considers Skye.
A huge hard light falls across shifting hills.
This mind, contemptuous of miracles

and beggarly sentiment, illuminates
a healthy moderation. But I hear
like a native dog notes beyond his range

the modulations of a queer music
twisting his huge black body in the pain
that shook him also in raw blazing London.

FACE OF AN OLD HIGHLAND WOMAN

This face is not the Mona Lisa's
staring from a submarine
greenness of water. There's no grace
of any Renaissance on the skin

but rocks slowly thrust through earth
a map with the wind going over stone
beyond the mercies of Nazareth.
Here is the God of fist and bone

a complex twisted Testament
two eyes like lochs staring up
from heather gnarled by a bare wind
beyond the art and dance of Europe.

THE CLEARANCES

The thistles climb the thatch. Forever
this sharp scale in our poems,
as also the waste music of the sea.

The stars shine over Sutherland
in a cold ceilidh of their own,
as, in the morning, the silver cane

cropped among corn. We will remember this.
Though hate is evil we cannot
but hope your courtier's heels in hell

are burning: that to hear
the thatch sizzling in tanged smoke
your hot ears slowly learn.

IT IS THE OLD

It is the old
who get up in the night to build the fires for the young.
Their gods, they imagine, are disposed
in a leisurely lazy heaven and prolong
a Norman sleep against the cold
and bitter frost.

And so they set
a delicate structure of sticks, enfolded in this
fear of their power, idolatry of their poise.
Not knowing in Saxon dawns how the abyss
their precarious tilt of sticks steadily lights
is what their boys

dread in their beds,
while dreaming of lords they can serve
of brilliance courage and wit.
Roads are built on each nerve –
Roman and servile and powerful. Their needs
point to the fire in the night.

AT THE FIRTH OF LORNE

In the cold orange light we stared across
to Mull and Kerrera and far Tiree.
A setting sun emblazoned your bright knee
to a brilliant gold to match your hair's gold poise.

Nothing had changed: the world was as it was
a million years ago. The slaty stone
slept in its tinged and aboriginal iron.
The sky might flower a little, and the grass

perpetuate its sheep. But from the sea
the bare bleak islands rose, beyond the few
uneasy witticisms we let pursue
their desolate silences. There was no tree

nor other witness to the looks we gave
each other there, inhuman as if tolled
by some huge bell of iron and of gold,
I no great Adam and you no bright Eve.

THE LAW AND THE GRACE

It's law they ask of me and not grace.
'Conform,' they say, 'your works are not enough.
Be what we say you should be' even if
graceful hypocrisy obscures my face.

'We know no angels. If you say you do
that's blasphemy and devilry.' Yet I have
known some bright angels, of spontaneous love.
Should I deny them, be to falsehood true,

the squeeze of law which has invented torture
to bring the grace to a malignant head?
Do you want me, angels, to be wholly dead?
Do you need, black devils, steadfastly to cure

life of itself? And you to stand beside
the stone you set on me? No, I have angels. Mine
are free and perfect. They have no design
on anyone else, but only on my pride

my insufficiency, imperfect works.
They often leave me but they sometimes come
to judge me to the core, till I am dumb.
Is this not law enough, you patriarchs?

'NOTHING HUMAN'

'Nothing human is alien to me.'
But what if he is alien to it?
What if somewhere deep beyond the light
something ungraspable is waiting. He

stretches his hand out, but it won't come.
It doesn't even snarl. Yet he feels
a certain eeriness, as of strange skills
he did not know of : and to speak its name

is beyond art, beyond the possible.
Beggars may grovel in a bowl of light
or the silks reveal the cold aristocrat
or the little bourgeois clicking at his till.

But what if beyond all this, beyond the frontier –
Danube of dance – the marshes strangely stir
and the early morning has a sinister air.
This is beyond the artifice of fire

or hot desire or will, a slight shift
in landscape or in mind, a way it veers
untellably off its axis, and the lyres
untellably off their strings. This isn't loved

but purely alien, opaquely human.
It might be better if the wolf should come
loping in careless liberty to Rome
than this which is so alien and unroman.

THE SQUIRREL

The squirrel lay on the cold stone
seeming at first a rat, so dead and brown
I didn't dare go near it, for the shudder
of cold distaste and a hot primitive fear.

Flattened it lay, splayed on that cold distaste
as if a car had flung it, like the waste
spun from a turning axle. It was then
someone picked it up so limp and brown

and showed us it was squirrel. Thus at ease
because of the clear dryness of the trees
my eyes could study it. Quite still and pale
I twitched along it from the head to tail

but the tail was missing. And I thought with fear.
What death destroyed you? What has bitten there?
Or tugged it clear, whether alive or dead?
A seesaw forest shivered in my head

thinking – a ferret. Or a boy perhaps
in all that darkness, all the sparkling gaps
alive with venomous green. Till I looked down
and touched it, trembling. Empty and quite brown

it did not shiver. Only I remained
with shock on shock biting my shaking mind
and thinking: Dear one, better to be man,
though pain assaults us, from the trees come down.

SPRING WEDDING

Step out, my dear, down the aesthetic aisles
The wind is pulling at your bridal veils.
The black wears roses, and the shoes stream out
dazzle of roses from their mirrors' light.

Ethics of minister, and the standing choir
fix you this moment in your own quiet shire.
The cameras click for albums to be stored
of billowing lady and her pin-striped lord.

Existence threatens as in veils you go
through gales of spring which tug your furbelow
Neat black, proud white, the angel must be held
by a black anchor on a shadowy field.

THE CEMETERY NEAR BURNS'
COTTAGE

Tombs of the Covenanters nod together
grey heads and obstinate. They saw them come
the silver horsemen meditating murder
but stood there quietly to the beating drum
of God and psalm, the heart's immaculate order.

So now I see them as the churchyard turns
red in the evening light. They did not know
that moral milk turns sour, and something churns
inside the stony cask. This churchyard now
flickers with light, untameably with Burns,

the secret enemy within the stone,
the hand which even here stings its hot whip
in glittering rays from socketed bone to bone.
In such fixed Eden did his changing shape
unlock their teeth from what they'd bravely won.

HUME

More than this I do not love you,
Hume of the reasonable mind.
There was an otter crossed the sound,
a salmon in his cold teeth.

The mist came down. Between two capes
there was no road. There was a French
salon, an adoring wench.
He picked the salmon with his teeth.

Delicate Hume who swims through all
the daring firths of broken Scotland,
there were no roads across the land.
The causes, like old fences, yawned

gravely over wit and port.
Diplomacies are what displace
the inner law, the inner grace,
the Corrievreckan of bad art.

RYTHM

They dunno how it is. I smack a ball
right through the goals. But they dunno how the words
get muddled in my head, get tired somehow.
I look through the window, see. And there's a wall
I'd kick the ball against, just smack and smack.
Old Jerry he can't play, he don't know how,
not now at any rate. He's too flicking small.
See him in shorts, out in the crazy black.
Rythm, he says, and ryme. See him at back.
He don't know nuthing about Law. He'd fall
flat on his face, just like a big sack,
when you're going down the wing, the wind behind you
and crossing into the goalmouth and they're roaring
the whole great crowd. They're up on their feet cheering.
The ball's at your feet and there it goes, just crack.
Old Jerry dives – the wrong way. And they're jearing
and I run to the centre and old Bash
jumps up and down, and I feel great, and wearing
my gold and purpel strip, fresh from the wash.

SO MANY NAMES

So many names cut in the grey stone –
Angus and Norman, Mary, Margaret, Iain –
deep alphabet of dying: and the green

fattened by bones, as thin as Gaelic airs.
I see the dead lean over rusty wires
or resting shoulders against marble byres

and puffing clouds of smoke as they discuss
with the carved angels how the hay and grass
are rich and green where the cold thistle was.

PREPARATION FOR A DEATH

Have I seen death conquered at last in you
dying by inches, yet with lucid sight
examining its gains? The world was new
and sparkled with a gay Renaissance wit,

but now the Reformation has set in.
A narrow Luther hedges the red blood
and bellows from his pulpit like a pain.
The blossoming angels in their painted red

are withered into devils. All the pardons
are snatched inhospitably from your open wound
and nothing's left but a creeping host of sins
which you consider with a bleak mind

on the very edge of nothingness looking out,
like Drake going off beyond all human shores
and no Elizabeth to dub you knight
but mind itself to open its black doors.

ENCOUNTER IN A SCHOOL CORRIDOR

Supposing today walking along this passage
in a flicker of gown Death were to turn and look
with his white skull face, raising his eyes from his book,
and I were to stare directly into that visage

which is almost over-learned and frightened too
as if to say: 'Surely not you as well.'
In this hygienic place without sound or smell
what would I, late cold Roman, say or do

but this perhaps: 'Always there was correction.
After the Fall, the careless summer leaves
must learn strict order, for the heart deceives
by wayward and incurious affection.

And the seasons always begin. There is no end
to the iron ring of law, the field of grace
whose shadows slant before the footballers.'
He then might show some pity as he turned

to face me down the dim-lit corridor
his arms so piled with books, face grained with thought,
and his slow legs remembering that riot
of flowering shadows and that youthful force.

To forget the dead. How to forget the dead
when they slowly sigh, walking about the rooms
where we are lying, deep in a white bed.
How to forget that with discoloured arms

they are searching drawers for their property –
a favourite ribbon, book – while we lie still
under the bedclothes lest they hear us cry,
and stuffing sheets in our round mouths, till

we are the dead, swathed in our tight linen,
and those who leave no shadow in the glass
stand at the door a moment, but refrain
from touching our white gravestones as they pass.

HIGHLANDERS

They sailed away into the coloured prints
of Balaclava, or at tall Quebec
you'll see them climbing almost native rock
in search of French and not of cormorants.

Abroad, they fought the silks and bright coats
while to their homes the prancing dandies came
on horses like Napoleon's, in the calm
(but clouds of snuff) of all their ruined boats,

them high on Nelson's topmasts looking over
a coloured sea at evening coming up
with complex tackle and harmonious rope
from pictured oceans and a roaring fire.

POEM IN MARCH

Old cans sparkle. Tie slaps at the chin.
The mind puts on its sword.
This is the country of the daffodil
and the new flannels, radiant and belled.

The drawn cheeks and the spiky knees
are suddenly tulips, roses,
an England and the Low Countries.
A map of shadows passes

out on the sixteenth century sea,
Raleigh to sail and Drake
beyond the monks of eternity
reading a winter book.

THE SONG

'Never again will we part.' So says the song.
So why should the heart be downcast when it hears
what for so many years it has learnt to long
for, most and tenderly. Why should the hours

suddenly seem to freeze on the clock
in their black monuments? And why should you
sit in the happy ending like a rock
when the sea and sky around you are so blue?

THE CHESS PLAYER

When the badness came he was playing chess again.
'Someone most dear to you,' they said, 'has died.'
He scouted round the board and picked the queen.
(What use are bishops, knights?) 'We found,' they cried,
'your brother dead. His wounds were in the side.'

'Not in the head?' he said, not looking up.
'In the head and heart as well,' they answered. He
moved the tall queen delicately as in hope
but the king escaped again. 'Did he say of me
anything hopeful?' he asked savagely,

moving a pawn, his head carved to the wood
the king was carved from. 'No,' they said. ' "Please tell
my brother this. Tell him I've understood
a very little." That's what he told us.' 'Well,
The chessboard tells me what of heaven or hell

I need to know and that's too much,' he cried,
shifting the queen. (The king escaped again.)
He smiled a little with the jaunty pride
one sometimes notices in desperate men.
'You see,' he said, 'when you came in just then

I had a vision of that very board.
They do not know, you see, none of them knows.
They're all quite evidently so far apart.
What do they know of each other? I dispose –
but each is wooden, in archaic pose.'

And then they saw (each one standing beside
the terrible trivial wrestler) with a start
that someone most dear to him indeed had died,
and stared at him grappling with his mental art,
and carefully made ready to depart.

THE WREATH

She broke the stalks clean off; stuck wire instead
just below the flower: then, in the wreath,
fitted the tall tulips, yellow and red.
There was nothing wrong with her: she would plainly
   breathe
for another decade. Her white busy head

was bowed in concentration on the wires
as if on needlework precise and pure.
A clear vocation had transformed desires
into a gaunt deftness, like a cure
for fires more feverish than the tulips' fires.

Her hands were not quite Dutch, not quite so slow
or peasant – heavy, used to earth alone.
But rather quick and veined and faintly sallow
as if inured to the eternal stone
on which the moving shadows ebb and flow.

A Fury rather in that florist's shop
snapping the stalks and fitting needles there
in a skilful motion without thought or hope
or any grief displacing her grey hair
next door to April and the neighbouring Co-op

and not considering how the hands will fail,
the needles cease, the bright embroidery halt,
the traffic whisper, and a strange voice wail.
This day in April without love or fault
she weaves a bouquet for that queer Miss Dale.

THE LONE RIDER

It's not the worst ones that things happen to.
Often across the countries of the mind
one sees the careless ones, carelessly riding through
a beautiful land, without dark cloud or wind,
almost like pictures ill luck can't pursue.

They laugh in taverns and they drink cool water,
they descend high mountains to the other side
in a curve of easiness language cannot utter,
they and the horses that they calmly ride
are quite inseparable in centaur weather.

But the others with their wagons all weighed down
by women's hysteria, furniture, design –
the Indians attack them, and at dawn
the wolves lope by them with their famished skin
shining a little in the morning's shine.

And finally they're cornered in a canyon
where the mountains rise around them. Water spent
and ammunition finished, they drive on,
lugging their wardrobes and their sweet sad scent.
A yellow light entombs the caravan

lit with bright flashes of the lone rider
who climbs the jagged mountains, and is still
one step ahead of wolves and Indian murder.
His tireless horse strides on. From hill to hill
they watch with love their thirsty soul's provider.

THE ANGLO-SAXON LECTURER GOES
TO THE CINEMA EVERY THURSDAY

Monogrammed lady with her loaded tray
picked out in spotlight. Masculine they were
the stony Saxons with their snow-swept hair
icy by masts. Now it is Thor's day

time of the weekly film. And, clang, it goes
hammer on anvil: and the sliding words.
This music gnashes like the edge of swords.
The usherette is not his Mrs Rose,

her creamy linen tipped at the red breast.
The trumpets sound. The foreign masked ones come
across the ford. Enough to strike one dumb
on Maldon field, where hearts will never rest.

'Courage is keener.' Godric of the shame. . . .
There was another Godric who was brave,
stood sword in hand. Did not deserve a grave
as enemy came in armour, masked men came

with volleys, then with swords. The curtain's green,
ripples like water. Linen one subsides.
Mrs Rose comes marching, Mrs Gray besides.
'No trouble, Mrs Gray, he's always clean,'

in sliding titles which accelerate
down parting curtains. Maldon's final stand.
'Go on. Go on.' The masked and threatening band
surges past channels, as the days in spate

plunge at each Thor's day, the doomed fighting ones,
forever going on. 'Courage more hard
as numbers lessen': and the plunging sword
penetrating flesh, recurrent moons

monogrammed with blood, the music rising
round breast, round armour, round its rippling green,
by Maldon fading from the steady screen
and easier drama perishably blazing.

'WHETHER BEYOND THE STORMY HEBRIDES'

Too simple an ending that,
that he should rise as the sun rises
out of the waters where it never set.
Too simple this pure art's hypothesis
transforming bones and flesh into light.

Beyond the Hebrides he idly swings
nudged from reef to reef, dissolving where
the goggle-eyed fish sways and stings.
The herring and the mackerel take care
of his blue eyes, his lounging wanderings,

deep in the seaweed of the sighing cry,
the vacant plop, while, randomly above,
the angel seagulls cross the hanging sky
in their waste kingdom without joy or love
the hungry judges of eternity,

cruising above the salt with bulging eyes,
their yellow claws tucked tight beneath their wings
now sinking and now rising while their cries
remember nothing but in mindless rings
nag each blue bouquet as it shifts and dies.

THE PROPOSAL

This is my hairy hand. I am a killer.
I laugh quietly at the gold skull ring.
I laugh quietly in my guarded cave.

Beware of me, beware of the ape in me
crouching in the darkness. I'll get away
and leave you when you are in your sickness.

What have I to do with the lame,
the white morning face, the weakness?
Enough of these in myself I tell you

enough of these. I have grown up with these.
I admire the hairy hand only,
my opposite, my denseness,

Jacob feeding from the dying mouth,
bee at the white flower. I am an ape man,
evil all through. I know the desert, ·

the sinuous manoeuvrings, the image
which makes me sick. How can I give you
water or manna? Bending, all I see

is all hair, this true hairy hand.
The sign on the finger a blue sun
sparkling ahead of reason.

ENVOI

Remember me when you come into your kingdom.
Remember me, beggar of mirrors, when you are confirmed
in the sleep of fulfilment on the white pillow.

Remember me who knock at the window,
who hirple on my collapsing stick, and know
the quivering northern lights of nerves.

Remember me in your good autumn.
I in my plates of frost go
among the falling crockery of hills

stones, plains, all falling and falling.
In my winter of the sick glass remember
me in your autumn, in your good sleep.